NORTHWEST
Dryland Wildflowers
Sagebrush–Ponderosa

Dana Visalli ◆ **Walt Lockwood** ◆ **Derrick Ditchburn**

hancock

house

ISBN 0-88839-517-5

Cataloging in Publication Data

Visalli, Dana, 1948-
    Northwest dryland wildflowers: sagebrush-ponderosa / Dana Visalli,
Walt Lockwood, Derrick Ditchburn.

(Northwest wildflower series)
Includes index.
ISBN 0-88839-517-5

    1. Wild flowers—Northwest, Pacific--Identification. I. Lockwood, Walt,
1938- II. Ditchburn, Derrick, 1934- III. Title. IV. Series.

QK144.V582 2005   582'.13'09795   C2004-901828-0

Printed in South Korea—PACOM

Editor: Dana Visalli
Photography: Dana Visalli, Walt Lockwood, Derrick Ditchburn,
            David Hancock, Don McPhee & Mildred McPhee
Production: Rick Groenheyde, Laura Michaels, Theodora Kobald

Published simultaneously in Canada and the United States by

HANCOCK HOUSE PUBLISHERS LTD.
19313 Zero Avenue, Surrey, B.C. Canada V3S 9R9
(604) 538-1114 Fax (604) 538-2262

HANCOCK HOUSE PUBLISHERS
1431 Harrison Avenue, Blaine, WA U.S.A 98230-5005
(604) 538-1114 Fax (604) 538-2262

Website: **www.hancockhouse.com**
Email: **sales@hancockhouse.com**

Contents

Introduction

Welcome to the surprisingly attractive world of dryland wildflowers. Even dry land is wet in the spring, and our inland wildflowers take advantage of this moisture to bloom in profusion between April and July. This little book will help you identify the most common flowering species in the Inland Northwest.

Sometimes there are many look-alike species within a particular closely related group of plants. Two examples in this book are the lupines and the milkvetches. There are at least 20 species of lupines and 80 species of milkvetches in the Pacific Northwest. We will have to be satisfied in this book just to recognize these larger groups, and realize we don't know for sure exactly what species we are enjoying at any given moment.

Technical terms are avoided in the plant descriptions wherever possible; still a few do creep in. **Compound leaves** refers to leaves that are divided into a number of separate leaflets. If the leaflets are all joined together at a common point, like the fingers on a hand, they are **palmately compound**. If they are joined in twos opposite one another, they are **pinnately compound. Corolla** refers to all the petals of a flower, taken together. **Sepals** are the bracts below the petals that covered the flower bud before it opened. In the Lily Family, the sepals are often just as colorful as the petals; the two together are then referred to as **tepals**. The flowers of the Composite Family (also known as the Aster Family) are composed of many tiny flowers all combined into a circular **composite head**. What look like the petals in this group—think of what appear to be petals on a sunflower—are actually tiny flowers in their own right, called **ray flowers**. The center of a sunflower (and of many other composites) is made up of tiny **disk flowers**.

That should be enough to get you started. Whatever the demands and aspirations of your busy life, don't forget to enjoy the flowers.

MOCK-ORANGE
Philadelphus lewisii

Plant: Erect, loosely branched shrub mostly 1.5-2.5 m tall.

Flower: Fragrant, white, in clusters at branch ends, the 4 petals 10-20 mm long.

Leaves: Opposite, elliptic, sometimes serrate, 2.5-7 cm by 1-4 cm, with three major veins.

Habitat: Sage-steppe to ponderosa forest, in gullies and on cliffs.

Range: B.C. to California.

ROSACEAE · ROSE FAMILY
BITTER CHERRY
Prunus emarginata

Plant: Shrub or tree 2-10 m tall.

Flower: 5-10 white flowers at branch tips, petals rounded, 5-7 mm long.

Fruit: 5-10 pea-sized red cherries at branch tips, very bitter.

Leaves: Elliptic, 3-8 cm long, bluntly serrate, with 2 glands at base of stem.

Habitat: Varied and erratic, from streambanks to dry hills.

Range: B.C. to California.

PEARLY EVERLASTING
Anaphalis margaritacea

Plant: Perennial 20-90 cm tall, erect, unbranched, with a leafy stem.

Flower: A 3-10 cm wide cluster of small, white, papery, composite heads.

Leaves: Narrow, alternating up the stem, green above and white-woolly below.

Habitat: Meadows, forest openings, roadsides.

Range: Alaska to Oregon.

LYALL'S MARIPOSA LILY, HAIRY CAT'S EAR
Calochortus lyallii

Plant: Thin, erect perennial 10-50 cm high, with a single stalk and single stem leaf.

Flower: 3 ovate, fringed petals up to 3 cm long with purple crescent near the base.

Leaves: Usually one narrow leaf 10-30 cm long on stem, and a small, bract-like leaf near the flowers.

Habitat: Sage-steppe and ponderosa pine forest.

Range: B.C. to Yakima Co, Washington.

COMPOSITAE · COMPOSITE FAMILY

LOW PUSSYTOES

Antennaria dimorpha

Plant: Dwarf, grayish, matted perennial to 8 cm high.

Flower: Small (5 mm wide), whitish composite heads have only disk flowers.

Leaves: Leaves numerous, narrow and silky-hairy.

Habitat: Dry, open places in lowlands and foothills.

Range: B.C. to Oregon.

ROSACEAE · ROSE FAMILY

COLUMBIA HAWTHORN

Crataegus columbiana

Plant: A straggling shrub to small tree, 1-4 m tall, armed with slender thorns 4-7 cm long.

Flower: 5 white, rounded petals 5-8 mm long, flowers in clusters at branch tips.

Fruit: Red fruits are apple-like, 1 cm wide.

Leaves: Ovate or obovate, 2.5-6 cm long, serrate, and hairy on both surfaces.

Habitat: Meadows and streams to dry hillsides.

Range: B.C. to Oregon.

7

RHAMNACEAE · BUCKTHORN FAMILY
SNOWBRUSH
Ceanothus velutinus

Plant: A sprawling, spice-scented evergreen shrub to 30 m tall.

Flower: Small (1-3 mm) white flowers in compact clusters at branch tips, very fragrant.

Leaves: Ovate, 5-10 cm long, strongly 3-veined from base, very shiny on top, finely serrate.

Habitat: Sage-steppe to ponderosa forests.

Range: B.C. to California.

CONVOLVULACEAE · MORNING-GLORY FAMILY
FIELD MORNING-GLORY
Convolvulvus arvensis

Plant: Prostrate perennial from spreading rhizomes, stems trailing, 20-200 cm long.

Flower: Corolla white to pink, 1.5-2.5 cm long, 1-2 flowers in each leaf axil.

Leaves: Arrow-shaped, 2-6 cm long, alternate along the creeping stem.

Habitat: Roadsides, disturbed meadows and fields.

Range: Originally from Europe, now widespread in North America.

WHITE SHOOTING STAR
Dodecatheon dentatum

Plant: Perennial 15-40 cm tall.

Flower: 2-12 white flowers with yellow centers at top of leafless stalk, the reflexed petals 12-20 mm.

Leaves: All basal, ovate and toothed, 3-10 cm long, 2-6 cm wide.

Habitat: Mostly along streams, lowlands to Douglas-fir forests.

Range: B.C. to Oregon.

WHITE WATER BUTTERCUP
Ranunculus aquatilis

Plant: Rooted, spreading, aquatic perennial with floating flowers.

Flower: 5 white petals, often yellow at the base, each 5-10 mm long, flowers solitary in leaf axils.

Leaves: Submerged leaves divided into linear segments, floating leaves deeply 3-lobed.

Habitat: In ponds and sluggish streams, from lowlands to midelevations.

Range: Throughout much of North America.

9

CUT-LEAF FLEABANE

Erigeron compositus

Plant: Taprooted perennial 3-25 cm tall.

Flower: 1-10 composite heads with white to pink ray flowers and yellow centers.

Leaves: Small and mostly basal, finely once or twice divided into finger-like lobes.

Habitat: Dry, sandy to rocky places from low to high elevations.

Range: Alaska to California.

THREADLEAVED FLEABANE

Erigeron filifolius

Plant: Upright to spreading perennial 10-50 cm, with hairs lying flat on upper stems.

Flower: One to many composite heads, the rays blue to pink or white, the centers yellow.

Leaves: Linear, thread-like leaves 2-8 cm long, with finely appressed hairs.

Habitat: Dry places in plains and foothills, often among sagebrush.

Range: B.C. to California.

HOARY ASTER
Machaeranthera canescens

Plant: Branching biennial or perennial 10-50 cm tall.

Flower: A small composite, the rays white to blue, the center yellow.

Leaves: Toothed, the lower linear oblanceolate, up to 10 cm long, the upper shorter and linear.

Habitat: Dry open places in the plains and foothills, sometimes in disturbed sites.

Range: B.C. to California.

SHAGGY FLEABANE
Erigeron pumilis

Plant: An upright perennial 5-40 cm tall with shaggy, spreading hairs.

Flower: Pink, white, sometimes blue, with 50-100 narrow rays (petals).

Leaves: Linear-oblanceolate, 3-8 cm long, 3-8 mm wide, abundant on stems.

Habitat: Open places in the plains and foothills, often among sagebrush.

Range: B.C. to California.

11

WHITE VIRGINS-BOWER
Clematis ligusticifolia

Plant: A woody climbing vine to 20 m long.

Flower: Few to many in leaf axils, no petals, but the 4 white sepals are petal-like, 6-15 mm long.

Fruit: Seeds with long, feathery appendages.

Leaves: Opposite, pinnately compound with 5-7 ovate and serrate leaflets, each 3-6 cm long.

Habitat: Sage-steppe to lower forests, where at least vernally moist.

Range: B.C. to California.

POLYGONACEAE · BUCKWHEAT FAMILY

SNOW BUCKWHEAT
Eriogonum niveum

Plant: Matted perennial from a woody base, the flowering stems to 10-40 cm tall.

Flower: Very small, white to pink, brown with age, in small clusters along upright stem.

Leaves: Basal, ovate-elliptic, gray-hairy, 1.5-6 cm long, 1-3 cm wide.

Habitat: Sage-steppe to ponderosa forest.

Range: B.C. to Oregon.

PHILADELPHIA FLEABANE
Erigeron philadelphicus

Plant: Upright perennial 20-70 cm tall.

Flower: A pink to white composite head, the rays (petals) many and narrow.

Leaves: Basal leaves oblanceolate, 5-15 cm by 1-3 cm, stem leaves smaller, clasping stem.

Habitat: Moist, often disturbed sites at low to moderate elevations.

Range: Throughout much of North America.

CUSHION FLEABANE
Erigeron poliospermus

Plant: Small, taprooted, tufted perennial to 15 cm tall.

Flower: Pink to purple, 15-45 rays (petals), each composite flower solitary on the stem.

Leaves: Mostly in basal tufts, linear-oblanceolate, 3-8 cm by 5-12 mm.

Habitat: Dry places in plains and foothills, often among sagebrush.

Range: B.C. to Oregon.

13

WAX CURRANT
Ribes cereum

Plant: Thornless shrub .5-2 m tall.

Flower: Small pink or white tubular flowers .5-1 cm long, blooming in early spring.

Leaves: Fan-shaped, 1.5-2.5 cm, usually shallowly 3- or 5-lobed and serrate.

Habitat: Sage-steppe to dry midelevation openings.

Range: B.C. to California.

FOOL'S ONION
Brodiaea hyacinthina

Plant: 25-60 cm tall, with a cluster of white flowers atop a naked stem.

Flower: 3-20 white flowers, sometimes tinged with blue, tepals 10-16 mm long.

Leaves: 1-2 narrow leaves attached near base, up to 40 cm long and 3-10 mm wide.

Habitat: Grassy, often rocky open flats and moist meadows, lowlands to midmontane.

Range: B.C. to California.

CAPRIFOLIACEAE · HONEYSUCKLE FAMILY

BLUE ELDERBERRY
Sambucus cerulea

Plant: Shrub 2-5 m tall, with pithy, light-colored twigs and stems.

Flower: Small and white, crowded together in flat-topped clusters 10-20 cm across.

Fruit: Clusters of small, powder-blue, round fruits.

Leaves: Opposite one another on stem, each leaf divided into 5-9 lanceolate leaflets.

Habitat: Valleys, open slopes and roadsides.

Range: B.C. to California.

CRUCIFERAE · MUSTARD FAMILY

SPRING WHITLOW-GRASS
Draba verna

Plant: A very small annual 1-10 cm tall.

Flower: The 4 tiny (1-2.5 mm) petals are white, and so deeply lobed as to appear to be 8 in number.

Leaves: 1-2.5 mm long, oblanceolate and hairy, basal and rosulate (forming a circular tuft).

Habitat: Sage-steppe and ponderosa pine forest.

Range: Throughout much of North America.

15

MEADOW DEATH CAMAS
Zigadenus venenosus

Plant: Narrow, upright, grass-like perennial 20-50 cm tall.

Flower: White, the 6 tepals 4-5 mm long, the flowers many in rather dense, upright clusters.

Leaves: Grass-like, mostly basal, 10-30 cm long and 3-6 mm wide, keeled on underside.

Habitat: Sage-steppe to mountain meadows with adequate moisture.

Range: B.C. to Oregon.

LILIACEAE · LILY FAMILY

ELEGANT DEATH CAMAS
Zigadenus elegans

Plant: A narrow, upright perennial 30-60 cm tall.

Flower: 6 greenish yellow, spreading tepals 3-5 mm long, 10-20 flowers in an erect spike.

Leaves: Long and narrow, mostly basal, clasping the stem, 15-30 cm in length and 3-13 mm wide.

Habitat: Open grasslands to forest meadows.

Range: Alaska to Oregon.

RANUNCULACEAE · BUTTERCUP FAMILY

YELLOW-WHITE LARKSPUR
Delphinium xanthifolium

Plant: Single-stemmed, upright perennial 30-80 cm tall.

Flower: Yellow white, 1 cm wide and 1.5-2.5 cm long including the spur, the stem 2-10 flowered.

Leaves: Few in number, round in outline, 2-7 cm wide, deeply divided into narrow lobes 1-2 mm wide.

Habitat: Grassy hillsides and ponderosa pine forests.

Range: East-slope foothills of central Washington.

LEGUMINOSAE · PEA FAMILY

FRECKLED MILKVETCH
Astragalus leibergii

Plant: A spreading perennial 10-40 cm tall.

Flower: A white to pink pea-like flower 8-18 mm long, with 10-30 flowers crowded together, the reddish seed pod 1-3 cm long.

Leaves: Pinnately compound, with 11-19 obovate leaflets, each 8-15 mm long.

Habitat: Sage-steppe to alpine ridges.

Range: Washington to California.

POPCORN-FLOWER
Plagiobothrys figuratus

Plant: Erect, branching annual 10-40 cm tall.

Flower: White with a yellow center, fragrant, 5-10 mm wide, blooming continuously at top of stem.

Leaves: Relatively few, the lowest ones opposite on the stem, linear, 2-4 cm long, 2-4 mm wide.

Habitat: Meadows, low ground, moist fields.

Range: B.C. to Oregon.

SAGEBRUSH STICKSEED
Hackelia arida

Plant: An upright, hairy perennial 20-80 cm tall.

Flower: 5 white petals with a yellow center, 6-12 mm wide, flowers bloom progressively up the stem.

Fruit: 4 prickly nutlets per flower.

Leaves: Basal leaves long and narrow, 5-20 cm by 2-10 mm, the few stem leaves smaller.

Habitat: Shrub-steppe and open ponderosa woodland.

Range: Washington.

18

GRAY CRYPTANTHA

Cryptantha leucophaea

Plant: Hairy perennial with clustered stems 15-40 cm tall.

Flower: 5 white petals with a light yellow center, flowers 5-10 mm across, crowded at stem tips.

Leaves: Oblanceolate, 5-10 cm long and 3-10 mm wide, basal and alternate up the stem.

Habitat: Dry, sandy places, often near the Columbia River.

Range: B.C. to Oregon.

PALE EVENING-PRIMROSE

Oenothera pallida

Plant: A narrow, upright perennial 10-50 cm tall.

Flower: Petals white, 1.5-3 cm, fragrant, the sepals turned to one side.

Leaves: Linear, 2-6 cm long, 2-5 mm wide.

Habitat: Sandy and gravelly soil, often on dunes and roadcuts.

Range: Washington and Oregon.

SPRINGBEAUTY
Claytonia lanceolata

Plant: A delicate, fleshy perennial 5-20 cm tall.

Flower: 3-20 white to pink flowers above the paired leaves, the 5 petals 7-12 mm long.

Leaves: Basal leaves few or absent, the 2 stem leaves opposite, elliptic, 1.5-7 cm by 5-20 mm.

Habitat: Sage-steppe to alpine slopes, usually where moist in early spring.

Range: B.C. to California.

THREAD-LEAVED SANDWORT
Arenaria capillaris

Plant: Perennial forming mats 5-20 cm wide and 10-20 cm tall, flower stems glandular.

Flower: 1-10 white flowers per stalk, petals rounded, 1 cm long, sepals purple-tinged.

Leaves: Linear, basal leaves many, 2-4 cm long, stem leaves in pairs, opposite one another.

Habitat: In open areas from sagebrush plains to subalpine slopes.

Range: Alaska to Oregon.

SERVICEBERRY, SASKATOONBERRY

Amelanchier alnifolia

Plant: A shrub or small tree 1-5 m tall.

Flower: Abundant, showy white flowers in clusters at branch tips, each with 5 petals 1-2 cm long.

Fruit: Purple to black pomes (apple-like) 5-10 mm in diameter, seedy, but edible and tasty.

Leaves: Oval, 2-4 cm long, toothed on the upper half.

Habitat: Open woods, canyons, hillsides, low to high elevations.

Range: Alaska to California

CHOKECHERRY

Prunus virginiana

Plant: Shrub or small tree, 1-5 m tall.

Flower: Numerous small white flowers (petals about 5 mm) in narrow, elongate clusters.

Fruit: Small red to black cherries in elongate clusters, edible but very astringent.

Leaves: Widely elliptic and finely serrate, 4-10 cm long.

Habitat: Open forests and grasslands, and in dry, rocky sites.

Range: Throughout much of North America.

21

DWARF HESPEROCHIRON

Hesperochiron pumilis

Plant: Low perennial 5-10 cm tall.

Flower: 5 white petals with yellow centers and purple penciling, one flower per stem.

Leaves: Basal, elliptic, to 7.5 cm by 2.5 cm.

Habitat: In meadows and on moist slopes from low to midelevations.

Range: Eastern Cascades, Washington.

TALL BUCKWHEAT

Eriogonum elatum

Plant: A perennial with a basal clump of large leaves and an upright stem 30-90 cm tall.

Flower: Many tiny white flowers clustered together in numerous small white heads, at the ends of long stalks.

Leaves: All basal, lanceolate to ovate, 8-20 cm long, on long stems.

Habitat: Sage-steppe to open mountain slopes, sometimes on disturbed ground.

Range: Washington to California.

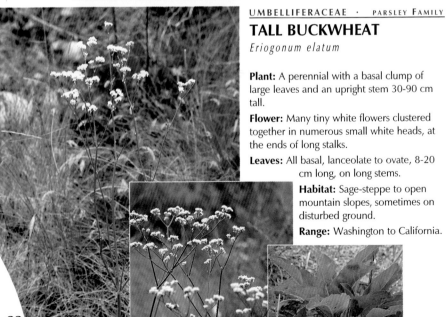

COMPOSITAE · COMPOSITE FAMILY
YARROW
Achillea millefolium

Plant: An erect, aromatic perennial 10-80 cm tall.

Flower: A 5-10 cm wide cluster of small, white composite flowers.

Leaves: Fern-like, finely divided and aromatic.

Habitat: Grasslands, meadows and forest edge, lowlands to alpine.

Range: Alaska to Oregon.

SCROPHULARIACEAE · FIGWORT FAMILY
HOT-ROCK PENSTEMON
Penstemon deustus

Plant: A low shrub with serveral stems from a woody base, 10-60 cm tall.

Flower: Dull white with purple guide lines inside, 8-20 mm long, flowers in loose, upright spikes.

Leaves: Oblanceolate to elliptic, usually toothed, sometimes in whorls, 2-6 cm long.

Habitat: Dry, open, often rocky places, from lowlands to midmountains.

Range: Washington to California.

23

WHITETOP, HOARY CRESS
Cardaria draba

Plant: Rhizomatous, spreading, erect perennial 10-50 cm tall.

Flower: Numerous small white flowers in crowded heads at top of stems, petals 3-4 mm long.

Leaves: Lanceolate, serrate, 4-10 cm long and 1-4 cm wide, 'eared' where they meet the stem.

Habitat: Moist open areas, typically where dry by summer.

Range: A Eurasian weed, now throughout western U.S.

UMBELLIFERACEAE · PARSLEY FAMILY

BIG BUCKWHEAT
Eriogonum heracloides

Plant: A spreading perennial with a woody base, 10-40 cm tall and 10-60 cm across.

Flower: Many very small (1-3 mm) cream, yellow or reddish flowers gathered in 5-20 round clusters.

Leaves: Basal, lanceolate, 2-8 cm by 2.5-10 mm, gray-hairy at least below.

Habitat: Sage-steppe and ponderosa to alpine ridges.

Range: B.C. to California.

24

POLEMONIACEAE · PHLOX FAMILY

TUFTED PHLOX
Phlox caespitosa

Plant: An ascending perennial from a woody base 5-15 cm tall.

Flower: Often solitary at the branch tips, corolla white, 1-2 cm wide, petals rounded.

Leaves: Linear, firm, sharp-tipped, 5-13 mm long and about .5 mm wide.

Habitat: Sage-steppe to ponderosa pine forest.

Range: B.C. to Oregon.

POLEMONIACEAE · PHLOX FAMILY

PRICKLY PHLOX
Leptodactylon pungens

Plant: A small branching shrub 10-60 cm tall.

Flower: White to pink tubular, solitary along stem, 5 petals 6-10 mm long, night-flowering.

Leaves: Compound, dissected into 3-7 very narrow, sharp-pointed segments 5-12 mm long.

Habitat: Deserts and plains to lower mountains.

Range: B.C. to Baja.

ORCHIDACEAE   ·   Orchid Family

WHITE LADIES-TRESSES
Spiranthes romanzoffiana

Plant: A narrow, upright perennial 5-30 cm tall.

Flower: White, 7-12 mm long, arranged in a dense spike of 2-4 vertically spiraling rows.

Leaves: Linear to narrowly oblong, 8-20 cm long and 5-10 mm wide, basal and low on stem.

Habitat: Moist to swampy areas.

Range: Alaska to California.

SAXIFRAGACEAE   ·   Saxifrage Family

BULBIFEROUS FRINGECUP
Lithophragma bulbifera

Plant: Annual 5-30 cm tall, with flower stems typically red.

Flower: Petals white to pink, 4-8 mm, deeply cleft, 2-8 flowers at top of almost leafless stalk.

Leaves: Mostly basal, ovate, 1-2 cm across, deeply cleft into 5 segments. There are tiny red bulblets at the base of the few stem leaves.

Habitat: Sage-steppe to open pondeosa and Douglas-fir forests.

Range: B.C. to California.

SAXIFRAGACEAE · SAXIFRAGE FAMILY

WOODLAND STAR

Lithophragma parviflora

Plant: An annual 10-40 cm tall, with flower stems typically green.

Flower: Petals white to pink, 5-10 mm, 3-5 cleft, 2-8 flowers at top of almost leafless stalk.

Leaf: Mostly basal, circular, 2-3 cm across, deeply divided into usually 5 segments.

Habitat: Sage-steppe to lower montane forest.

Range: B.C. to California.

SANTALACEAE · SANDALWOOD FAMILY

BASTARD TOADFLAX

Comandra umbellata

Plant: A perennial 5-35 cm tall, usually with several clustered stems.

Flower: White to pink, 3-7 mm long, clustered at top of stem.

Leaves: Elliptic, rather thick and fleshy, 4-40 mm long and 1-10 mm wide.

Habitat: Dry to moist, sandy open sites, lowlands to low mountains.

Range: Throughout North America.

WHITE TIDYTIPS
Layia glandulosa

Plant: A branching, hairy, spreading annual 5-44 cm tall.

Flower: A small, white composite head, with rays (petals) 4-15 mm long, three-lobed at the tip.

Leaves: Long and narrow, 1-6 cm by 1-6 mm, the lower toothed or lobed, the upper entire.

Habitat: Dry, open places in deserts and foothills.

Range: B.C. to Baja.

YELLOW-LEAVED IRIS
Iris chrysophylla

Plant: A rhizomatous perennial 10-60 cm tall, forming clumps up to 30 cm across.

Flower: 1 or 2, light yellow with darker veins, sepals 4.5-6.5 cm, the petals shorter.

Leaves: Those near ground 20-40 cm long and 3-5 mm wide, those on flower stem smaller, and opposite one another.

Habitat: Open ponderosa and Douglas-fir woods.

Range: Oregon to California.

LOW SANDWORT
Arenaria franklinii

Plant: A small perennial 3-8 cm tall, forming a spreading cushion.

Flower: White, congested in clumps at stem ends, petals 5-12 mm, sepals narrow, pointed.

Leaves: Linear and sharp-pointed, 1-3 cm.

Habitat: Sage-steppe and scablands in sand and rock.

Range: Washington to Oregon.

LARGE-SEEDED LOMATIUM
Lomatium macrocarpum

Plant: A low-growing perennial 5-20 cm tall.

Flower: The very small, white to purple flowers are in tight clusters on leafless stalks.

Leaves: Finely divided into fern-like segments, distinctly gray in color.

Habitat: Dry rocky ground at low to midelevations.

Range: B.C. to Oregon.

29

BITTERBRUSH, ANTELOPE-BUSH

Purshia tridentata

Plant: Stiffly branching shrubs 5-3 m tall.

Flower: 5 yellow petals, the numerous aromatic flowers are 1 cm wide.

Leaves: Small (1-2 cm), wedge-shaped leaves are 3-toothed at the tip.

Habitat: Shrub-steppe to ponderosa pine and juniper woodlands.

Range: B.C. to California.

TALL SAGEBRUSH

Artemisia tridentata

Plant: An erect, aromatic shrub mostly .5-6 m, distinctly grayish in color.

Flower: Very small (1 mm), yellow composite flower heads appear on an upright stalk in late summer.

Leaves: Wedge-shaped, 1.5-4 cm long and usually distinctly 3-toothed.

Habitat: Usually in dry plains and lowlands, occasionally subalpine.

Range: B.C. to Oregon.

WESTERN GROUNDSEL
Senecio integerrimus

Plant: A perennial 10-70 cm tall with solitary stems topped by multiple composite flowers.

Flower: 3-10 composite yellow heads at top of stalk, rays (petals) 6-15 mm long.

Leaves: Elliptic, 6-25 cm long, usually somewhat thick and hairy.

Habitat: Dry to rather moist open places and open woods.

Range: B.C. to Oregon.

RABBIT-BRUSH
Chrysothamnus nauseosus

Plant: An upright, gray-colored shrub 20-150 cm tall.

Flower: Numerous small, yellow composite heads bloom at stem tips in late summer.

Leaves: Linear, 2-7 cm long, finely gray-hairy.

Habitat: Dry, open places in valleys and foothills, occasionally higher.

Range: B.C. to Oregon.

WAVY-LEAVED MICROSERIS

Microseris troximoides

Plant: A perennial with a basal cluster of narrow leaves and dandelion-like flowers solitary on leafless stems, to 30 cm tall.

Flower: Composite heads made up of numbers yellow ray flowers (petals), 3-6 cm wide.

Leaves: Long and narrow, with wavy margins, all basal.

Habitat: Dry, open places in the lowlands and foothills.

Range: B.C. to California.

YELLOW BELL

Fritillaria pudica

Plant: A delicate, erect perennial 5-30 cm tall.

Flower: 1 or 2, yellow, the 6 tepals forming a pendent bell 10-25 mm long, fading to red.

Leaves: 2 and opposite, or 3-4 and semi-whorled, linear-oblanceolate, 3-16 cm long and 3-12 mm wide.

Habitat: Sage-steppe and dry grasslands from low to midelevations.

Range: B.C. to Oregon.

HORNSEED BUTTERCUP

Ranunculus testiculatis

Plant: A small annual to 2-10 cm tall.

Flower: On leafless stalks, petals yellow, 5-8 mm long, sepals green.

Fruit: The seed head forms an upright, cylindric cluster about 1 cm tall.

Leaves: All basal, 1.5-4 cm long, once or twice divided into finger-like projections.

Habitat: Dry, often disturbed sites, in sagebrush.

Range: Introduced from Eurasia, now throughout the west.

OROBANCHACEAE · BROOMRAPE FAMILY

CLUSTERED BROOMRAPE

Orobanche fasciculata

Plant: A non-photosynthetic plant parasitic on sagebrush, the yellow or purple stems to 15 cm tall.

Flower: Yellow or purple, 15-30 mm long, tubular with 5 corolla lobes, flowers 1-10.

Leaves: Reduced to small, ovate bracts on stem.

Habitat: Open areas in plains and foothills.

Range: B.C. to Oregon.

33

BARESTEM LOMATIUM
Lomatium nudicaule

Plant: A single or multiple-stemmed perennial 10-80 cm tall.

Flower: Tiny yellow flowers gathered together into multiple small globose heads at tip of stem.

Leaves: Few, compound, with 3-30 oval, veiny leaflets that are 2-9 cm long and 1-6 cm wide.

Habitat: Sage-steppe to ponderosa pine forest.

Range: B.C. to Oregon.

SPRING GOLD, SWALE DESERT PARSLEY
Lomatium ambiguum

Plant: A perennial 10-80 cm tall.

Flower: The tiny yellow flowers are clumped together in 5-20 round, spreading heads.

Leaves: Several times divided, the longer segments 1-8 cm by 1-5 mm.

Habitat: Dry, open, often rocky soil from low to moderate elevations.

Range: B.C. to Oregon.

GOLDEN CURRANT
Ribes aureum

Plant: Erect, thornless shrubs 1-3 m tall.

Flower: Tubular, the 5 spreading yellow petals 5 mm long, 5-18 flowers clumped together, fragrant.

Leaves: Ovate, deeply 3-lobed and bluntly serrate, 2-5 cm wide.

Habitat: Moist areas in sage-steppe and ponderosa pine forest.

Range: Washington to California.

NARROW-LEAVED DESERT PARSLEY
Lomatium triternatum

Plant: A taprooted perennial 10-80 cm tall.

Flower: Tiny yellow flowers clumped together in round heads at top of stem.

Leaves: Mostly basal, 2-3 cleft into long, narrow final segments 1-10 cm long.

Habitat: Open slopes and meadows, in dry to fairly moist soil.

Range: B.C. to Oregon.

YELLOW EVENING PRIMROSE
Oenothera strigosa

Plant: A narrow, upright perennial 20-100 cm tall.

Flower: Yellow, with 4 petals 1-2 cm long and 4 reflexed sepals 10-15 mm long.

Leaves: Narrowly elliptic, progressively smaller up stem, the larger ones 5-10 cm by 1-2.5 cm.

Habitat: Meadows and streambanks, from steppe to lower mountains.

Range: B.C. to Oregon.

COMMON BLADDERWORT
Utricularia vulgaris

Plant: Aquatic, free-floating, carnivorous perennials, equipped with small bladder-traps on leaves to catch small invertebrates, plants flower above water.

Flower: Yellow, two-lipped, 1-2 cm long, emerging from water on a long, upright stem.

Leaves: Numerous, alternate, compound, divided into fine, linear, fork-like segments.

Habitat: Ponds, lakes, marshes and slow-moving streams.

Range: Alaska to Oregon.

VIOLACEAE · VIOLET FAMILY

VALLEY YELLOW VIOLET
Viola nuttallii

Plant: A low perennial 4-15 cm tall.

Flower: 5-15 mm long, petals yellow, the lower purple-penciled, the upper brownish on back.

Leaves: Basal, ovate to elliptic, 2-10 cm long, 1-5 cm wide.

Habitat: In dry to vernally moist open areas from sage-steppe to Douglas-fir forest.

Range: B.C. to Oregon.

SCROPHULARIACEAE · FIGWORT FAMILY

YELLOW PENSTEMON
Penstemon confertus

Plant: A perennial with a woody base, 10-50 cm tall.

Flower: White to pale yellow, tubular, 8-12 mm long, in several clusters on upper stem.

Leaves: Elliptic, entire, basal ones to 15 cm long and 2.5 cm wide, stem leaves opposite.

Habitat: Moist meadows and open areas, along streams.

Range: B.C. to Oregon.

37

HOOKER'S BALSAMROOT
Balsamorhiza hookeri

Plant: A taprooted perennial 5-40 cm tall.

Flower: 1-10 yellow composite sunflower-like heads on long stalks, rays (petals) 1.5-4 cm long.

Leaves: Spear-shaped, 10-40 cm long, deeply lobed into fern-like segments.

Habitat: Dry, rocky ground in lowlands and foothills.

Range: Washington to Oregon.

TANSYLEAF EVENING-PRIMROSE
Oenothera tanacetifolia

Plant: A tufted perennial 10-20 cm tall.

Flower: 4 yellow petals 10-16 cm long, 4 reflexed sepals, 8 stamens.

Leaves: All basal, lanceolate, 5-20 cm long, 1-3.5 cm wide, deeply cleft into narrow lobes.

Habitat: Vernally moist soil from sage-steppe to ponderosa forests.

Range: Washington to Oregon.

ARROWLEAF BALSAMROOT

Balsamorhiza sagittata

Plant: A taprooted perennial 20-80 cm tall.

Flower: 1-30 yellow composite sunflower-like heads on long stalks, rays (petals) 3-8 cm.

Leaf: 10-30 cm long, distinctly arrowhead shaped, gray-hairy.

Habitat: Dry shrub-steppe to open ponderosa forest.

Range: B.C. to Oregon.

GRAY HORSEBUSH

Tetradymia canescens

Plant: Shrubs 20-60 cm tall, with leaves and twigs conspicuously white-woolly.

Flower: Composite, yellow, disk flowers only (no petals) clustered at branch tips.

Leaves: Linear to oblanceolate, 1 to 3 cm long and 1-4 mm wide, gray-hairy.

Habitat: Dry, open places in the foothills and plains.

Range: B.C. to California.

MULE'S EARS
Wyethia amplexicaulis

Plant: 30-80 cm tall taprooted perennial.

Flower: Typically 1 larger and 2 smaller composite heads per stalk, rays (petals) 2.5-5 cm.

Leaves: Elliptic and shiny, 20-60 cm long and 5-16 cm wide, both basal and on flower stem.

Habitat: Open hills and meadows , often where there is some spring moisture, foothills and low mountains.

Range: Washington.

LONG-LEAF HAWKSBEARD
Crepis acuminata

Plant: A taprooted perennial with 1-3 stems, 10-70 cm tall.

Flower: 10-100 yellow composite heads on top of tall stalk, rays 1-2 cm long.

Leaves: Elliptical, deeply cleft into long lobes, 10-40 cm long.

Habitat: Dry, open places from foothills to low mountains.

Range: Washington to Oregon.

COMMON SUNFLOWER
Helianthus annuus

Plant: A tall, narrow, erect annual .5-2 m tall.

Flower: The familiar sunflower of gardens, a large head with yellow rays and brown center.

Leaves: Ovate, serrate, alternate up stem, the lower ones quite large, 10-40 cm long.

Habitat: Open, dry to moderately moist places in prairies and foothills, disturbed ground.

Range: Native to western U.S. now widespread in North America and Eurasia.

LITTLE SUNFLOWER
Helianthella uniflora

Plant: Aa perennial 20-100 cm tall.

Flower: Yellow composite heads, ray flowers 2-4.5 cm long, one or few heads per stalk.

Leaves: Lanceolate to elliptic, 5-15 cm long, generally 3-nerved.

Habitat: Hillsides and open woods, low to midelevations.

Range: B.C. to Oregon.

41

CREEPING BUTTERCUP
Ranunculus repens

Plant: A low-growing, creeping perennial.

Flower: The yellow petals usually 5 but sometimes more, 7-17 mm long, stems hairy.

Leaves: 3-7 cm long, compound, triangular, the three main leaflets again lobed and serrate.

Habitat: Moist ground at lower elevations.

Range: Originally from Europe, now throughout much of the world.

SAGEBRUSH BUTTERCUP
Ranunculus glaberrimus

Plant: A low clumped perennial.

Flower: 5 yellow petals 8-15 mm long, often with a slight dent in the rounded tip.

Leaves: Mostly basal, shape variable, often with 3 deep notches, 1-2 cm long, 1-3 cm wide.

Habitat: Sage-steppe and ponderosa pine forest.

Range: B.C. to Oregon.

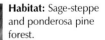

COMPOSITAE · COMPOSITE FAMILY

BROWN-EYED SUSAN
Gaillardia aristata

Plant: A taprooted perennial 10-70 cm tall.

Flower: 1 to 3 composite heads per stalk, the rays yellow, the center purple-brown.

Leaves: Narrowly elliptical, 5-12 cm long, 1-2.5 mm wide, entire to coarsely toothed.

Habitat: Prairies, dry meadows and other open places.

Range: B.C. to Oregon.

COMPOSITAE · COMPOSITE FAMILY

SALSIFY, GOATSBEARD
Tragopogon dubius

Plant: A taprooted biennial 30-100 cm tall.

Flower: Composite heads composed of numerous lemon-yellow ray flowers.

Fruit: Forms fluffy, dandelion-like seed head.

Leaves: Alternate and clasping on stem, grass-like, 10-30 cm long and 3-10 mm wide.

Habitat: Roadsides and other open, relatively dry places.

Range: Native of Europe, now throughout North America.

43

NORTHERN BUCKWHEAT
Eriogonum compositum

Plant: A matted perennial, the flower stalks 20-50 cm tall.

Flower: Flowers tiny, white to yellow, clustered in 5-10 loose heads at top of naked stem.

Leaves: Basal, spear-shaped, 7-25 cm long including stem, 1.5-5 cm wide, hairy below.

Habitat: On open, rocky slopes, lowlands to high mountains.

Range: Washington to Oregon.

STRICT BUCKWHEAT
Eriogonum strictum

Plant: A matted perennial from woody stems, flower stems 10-30 cm tall.

Flower: Small, yellow (sometimes white or pink), scattered along spreading stems or clustered together at the top.

Leaves: Ovate-elliptic, 5-25 mm long, on long petioles (leaf stems), hairy below.

Habitat: Sage-steppe to ponderosa pine forests.

Range: Washington to Oregon.

44

THYME BUCKWHEAT

Eriogonum thymoides

Plant: A low, tightly matted perennial from a woody base, 5-20 cm tall.

Flower: Very small, yellow to rose-red, clustered in tight heads at tip of stem.

Leaves: In whorls at woody branch tips, one whorl on flower stem, linear, 3-10 mm long.

Habitat: Sage-steppe and low rocky ridges.

Range: Central Washington to northern Oregon.

ROUND-HEADED BUCKWHEAT

Eriogonum sphaerocephalum

Plant: A spreading, branching shrub 10-70 cm tall.

Flower: Small yellow (occasionally white) flowers, clustered in rounded heads at stem tips.

Leaves: In whorls at branch tips, linear-oblanceolate, 1-3 cm by 3-6 mm, hairy below.

Habitat: Sage-steppe to openings in ponderosa and juniper forests.

Range: Washington to Oregon.

45

ST. JOHNSWORT
Hypericum perforatum

Plant: A single-to-several-stemmed, erect perennial 10-70 cm tall.

Flower: 5 spreading yellow petals 4-10 mm long, stamens numerous, flowers at stem tips.

Leaves: Narrowly elliptic, 1-3 cm long, 3-8 mm wide, with tiny clear spots in leaf blade.

Habitat: Meadows and fields, roadsides, disturbed ground.

Range: A native of Europe, now throughout the U.S.

GOLDENWEED
Haplopappus greenei

Plant: A low, broad shrub 10-30 cm tall.

Flower: 1-10 composite heads at the branch ends, the ray flowers 8-15 mm long.

Leaves: Oblanceolate, 1.5-3.5 cm long and 2-7 mm wide, alternate on woody stems of plant.

Habitat: Open or sparsely wooded slopes, low to high elevations.

Range: Washington to Oregon.

OREGON SUNSHINE
Eriophyllum lanatum

Plant: A hairy perennial 5-50 cm tall.

Flower: Many small sunflower-like composite heads, the ray flowers 1-2 cm long.

Leaves: Variable, 1-8 cm long, entire or divided, but always woolly.

Habitat: Dry, open places from the lowlands to moderate elevations.

Range: B.C. to Oregon.

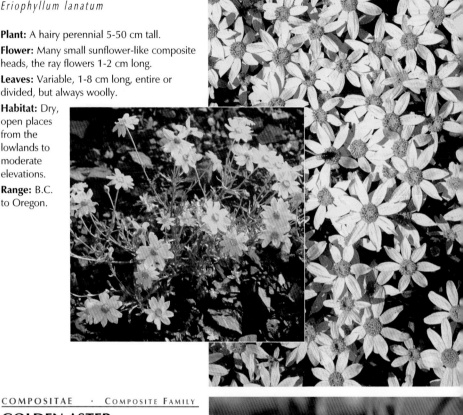

GOLDEN ASTER
Chrysopsis villosa

Plant: A tufted perennial from a woody base, 5-50 cm tall.

Flower: 1-10 yellow composite heads at top of stem, ray flowers 6-10 mm long.

Leaves: Oblanceolate, 2-5 cm long, 5-10 mm wide, alternate up stem.

Habitat: Dry, sunny, often sandy or gravelly sites.

Range: B.C. to Oregon.

47

STICKY CINQUEFOIL
Potentilla glandulosa

Plant: A glandular, erect perennial 10-40 cm tall, with one to several stems.

Flower: Pale yellow, the 5 petals 5-8 mm long, flowers borne in upright clusters at top of stem.

Leaf: Pinnately compound, with 5-9 oblong, serrate leaflets 1-3 cm long.

Habitat: Dry to moist open areas from lowlands to well up in mountains.

Range: B.C. to Oregon.

SLENDER CINQUEFOIL
Potentilla gracilis

Plant: An erect, generally hairy perennial 20-60 cm tall.

Flower: Yellow, the 5 petals 5-9 mm long, flowers in loose, flat-topped heads at stem tip.

Leaves: Palmately compound, with 7-9 oblong, deeply serrate leaflets 3-8 cm long.

Habitat: Moister areas in sagebrush desert to subalpine meadows.

Range: Alaska to Oregon.

BRITTLE CACTUS

Opuntia fragilis

Plant: Prostrate, forming low mats 5-20 cm tall, stems more-or-less cylindric, not flattened.

Flower: Many yellow petals and numerous yellow stamens, flowers 3-5 cm across.

Leaves: The leaves (actually the flattened stem) oblong, thick, 2-8 cm long, spines 1-3 cm.

Habitat: Sage-steppe to edge of ponderosa pine forest.

Range: B.C. to Oregon.

PRICKLY PEAR CACTUS

Opuntia polycantha

Plant: 10-30 cm tall, often forming mats 1-2 m across.

Flower: Yellow, sometimes tinged with red, 5-7 cm across, numerous yellow stamens within.

Leaves: The strongly flattened stems serve as leaves, 5-15 cm long, spines 1-5 cm.

Habitat: Dry, open areas from lowlands to lower mountains.

Range: B.C. to Oregon.

YELLOW FLEABANE, DESERT YELLOW DAISY
Erigeron linearis

Plant: A matted perennial 5-30 cm high.

Flower: 1 to several small yellow composite heads per stalk, ray flowers 4-11 mm long.

Leaves: Linear, 1.5-9 cm long, .5-3 mm wide, mostly basal.

Habitat: Dry, often rocky soil from foothills to midmountains.

Range: B.C. to California.

TALL OREGON GRAPE
Berberis aquifolium

Plant: A stiff, woody shrub 10-200 cm tall.

Flower: Inner sepals and petals yellow, 3-8 mm long, 5-40 flowers clustered at top of stem.

Fruits: Round, blue berry, 7-14 mm, edible.

Leaves: Pinnately compound, divided into 7-9 holly-like leaflets, each 3-8 cm long with spiny teeth.

Habitat: Dry grasslands and open woodlands.

Range: B.C. to Oregon.

PALE AGOSERIS
Agoseris glauca

Plant: A taprooted perennial 5-60 cm tall.

Flower: A single yellow dandelion-like composite head per stalk, ray flowers 1-3 cm long.

Leaves: All basal, linear-lanceolate or elliptic, 5-35 cm long, and 1-30 mm wide, entire or toothed.

Habitat: Meadows and other open places at all elevations.

Range: B.C. to Oregon.

PRIMULACEAE · PRIMROSE FAMILY

FRINGED LOOSESTRIFE
Lysimachia ciliata

Plant: A colonial perennial 20-120 cm tall from creeping rhizomes.

Flower: Yellow, the petals 1 cm long and pointed at the tip, fused together at the base.

Leaves: Opposite up stem, ovate, 5-15 cm long and 3-6 cm wide, the leaf stems long-hairy.

Habitat: Damp meadows, around ponds and lakes, and along streams.

Range: Scattered throughout temperate North America.

WESTERN WALLFLOWER
Erysimum occidentale

Plant: A gray-hairy, erect biennal 10-40 cm tall.

Flower: 4 bright yellow petals 6-10 mm long, 5-30 flowers together at stem tips.

Leaves: A basal rosette and leaves on stem, linear-oblanceolate, 4-8 cm long, 1-4 mm wide.

Habitat: Sage-steppe to ponderosa pine forest.

Range: Washington.

PERENNIAL SOWTHISTLE
Sonchus arvensis

Plant: A rhizomatous, spreading perennial 30-200 cm tall.

Flower: Yellow composite heads, rays numerous, flowers 3-12 in loose, erect clusters.

Leaves: Oblong, 6-40 cm long and 2-15 cm wide, lobed, toothed and prickly along edges.

Habitat: Disturbed open areas with some moisture.

Range: A cosmopolitan weed of European origin.

NARROW-LEAF GOLDENWEED
Haplopappus stenophyllus

Plant: A densely matted perennial from a woody base, growing 5-15 cm tall.

Flower: Yellow composite heads are solitary on stems, with 8-12 ray flowers (petals), and about as many smaller disk flowers.

Leaves: Linear, 1-2 cm long and 1-2 mm wide.

Habitat: Dry, open, rocky areas in the plains and foothills.

Range: Washington to California.

ANACARDIACEAE · SUMAC FAMILY

SUMAC
Rhus glabra

Plant: A small to large shrub .5-3 m tall.

Flower: Many tiny yellow flowers are crowded together in elongate, pyramidal clusters at stem tips, turning red in fruit.

Leaves: Compound, with 7-29 elliptical leaflets 5-12 cm long, turn deep red in the fall.

Habitat: Dry, scrubby areas in plains and foothills.

Range: throughout much of North America.

53

POLYGONACEAE · BUCKWHEAT FAMILY

DOUGLAS BUCKWHEAT
Eriogonum douglasii

Plant: A low, matted shrub 5-15 cm tall.

Flower: Many small cream to yellow flowers (6-8 mm) gathered together in globose heads.

Leaves: Mostly basal, linear, 5-20 mm long and 1.5-3 mm wide, gray hairy, at least below, with a whorl of leaves midway on flower stem.

Habitat: Sage-steppe to ponderosa and juniper forests.

Range: Washington to California.

LOASACEAE · BLAZING-STAR FAMILY

BLAZING-STAR
Mentzelia laevicaulis

Plant: A taprooted perennial 20-100 cm tall.

Flower: Very showy, 5 yellow petals 2.5-8 cm long, stamens yellow and very numerous.

Leaves: Lanceolate, 5-15 cm long, deeply lobed.

Habitat: Deserts to low mountains, often in rocky soil.

Range: B.C. to California.

THOMPSON'S PAINTBRUSH
Castilleja thompsonii

Plant: A perennial with several to many erect stems 10-40 cm tall.

Flower: Paintbrush flowers are composed in part of petal-like bracts, which are white to yellow in this species.

Leaves: Lower leaves linear and entire, upper leaves with 1-2 pairs of linear, divergent lobes.

Habitat: Sage-steppe and grasslands.

Range: B.C. and Washington.

BEARDED OWLCLOVER
Orthocarpus barbatus

Plant: An erect annual 5-25 cm tall with one to several stems.

Flower: Corolla yellow, 1-1.2 cm long, flowers clustered in leaf axils near top of stem.

Leaves: Narrow and entire or deeply 3- to 5-cleft into narrow lobes, 2-4 cm long.

Habitat: Sage-steppe.

Range: Central Washington.

55

HOUND'S-TONGUE HAWKWEED
Hieracium cynoglossoides

Plant: An upright perennial 30-120 cm tall.

Flower: 2-20 yellow composite heads at top of long stalk, black, hairs at base of heads.

Leaves: Lanceolate-elliptic, the lowest the largest, 10-25 mm long and 1-3 mm wide, with stiff hairs.

Habitat: Dry, open places, mostly in the foothills.

Range: B.C. to Oregon.

PUCCOON
Lithospermum ruderale

Plant: A perennial 20-60 cm tall with a cluster of upright stems from a woody base.

Flower: Tubular yellow flowers crowded in the axils of the upper leaves, 15-30 mm long.

Leaf: Many, all on stems, lanceolate, 2-6 cm long and 2-6 mm wide.

Habitat: Dry shrub-steppe and meadows.

Range: B.C. to Oregon.

BUTTER-AND-EGGS

Linaria vulgaris

Plant: An upright, colonial perennial from creeping rhizomes, 20-80 cm tall.

Flower: Snapdragon-like, yellow with orange throat, 2-3.5 cm long, many crowded at top of stems.

Leaves: Abundant, alternate up stems, linear, 2-10 cm long, 1-5 mm wide.

Habitat: Sage-steppe, grasslands and disturbed areas.

Range: Mediterranean native, now throughout the west.

FIDDLENECK

Amsinckia retrorsa

Plant: Annual 5-50 cm tall, covered with stiff hairs.

Flower: Orange-yellow, tubular flowers are 5-8 mm long and 1-3 mm wide, with a touch of red in the throat.

Leaves: Oblong, 3-12 cm and 5-10 mm wide, stiffly hairy, at plant base and along stem.

Habitat: Dry, open places in plains and foothills.

Range: B.C. to Oregon.

COMMON MULLEIN
Verbascum thapsus

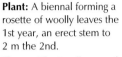

Plant: A biennal forming a rosette of woolly leaves the 1st year, an erect stem to 2 m the 2nd.

Flower: The 5 yellow petals are slightly asymmetrical, flowers many on elongated spike.

Leaves: Elliptic and densely hair, the lower 10-40 cm long, 3-12 cm wide, the upper smaller.

Habitat: Open, usually disturbed, areas at low to moderate elevations.

Range: Native of Eurasia, now throughout temperate North America.

ORCHIDACEAE · Orchid Family

YELLOW LADIES-SLIPPER
Cypripedium parviflorum

Plant: An upright perennial 15-40 cm.

Flower: Petals, including pouch, yellow, sepals brown or yellow, usually 1 flower per stem.

Leaves: Elliptic, 6-17 cm by 2-7 cm, parallel-veined, alternate on stem.

Habitat: Moist areas along streams, lakes and bogs.

Range: Throughout much of temperate North America, rare in our area.

LARGE-FLOWERED COLLOMIA

Collomia grandiflora

Plant: Narrow, erect annual 10-50 cm tall.

Flower: Flowers salmon to yellowish, 2-3 cm long, 2-10 clustered at top of stem.

Leaves: Leaves narrowly lanceolate, 2-9 cm long by 1-14 mm wide.

Habitat: Dry open areas to light woods, lowlands to midelevations.

Range: B.C. to Oregon.

TANSY

Tanacetum vulgare

Plant: A stout, erect, rhizomatous, aromatic perennial 40-150 cm tall.

Flower: A yellow-orange composite, button-like, with many heads in a flat-topped cluster.

Leaves: Compound, 10-20 cm long, divided into 7-13 narrow, deeply serrate leaflets.

Habitat: Roadsides, fields, waste places, river banks.

Range: Native of Eurasia, now common throughout temperate North America.

59

WILD CARROT, CHOCOLATE TIPS
Lomatium dissectum

Plant: A robust, taprooted perennial 30-150 cm tall at maturity.

Flower: Tiny brown or yellow flowers clumped in multiple round heads on a tall stalk.

Leaves: Large, basal and cauline, cleft several times into fine final segments, carrot-like.

Habitat: Dry, open, often rocky soil from low to moderate elevations.

Range: B.C. to Oregon.

RED-FLOWERING CURRANT
Ribes sanguineum

Plant: An erect, unarmed shrub 1-3 m tall with very showy flowers.

Flower: The sepals are a deep rose color, the corolla pink and 5-9 mm long, in clusters.

Leaves: Ovate, 2.5-6 cm wide, hairy below, 3- to 5-lobed and serrate.

Habitat: In open to wooded, moist to dry valleys of lower mountains.

Range: B.C. to Oregon.

POLEMONIACEAE · PHLOX FAMILY

SCARLET GILIA
Gilia aggregata

Plant: An upright biennial 20-100 cm tall, with 1 to several stems.

Flower: Red, tubular, generally numerous, 1.5-3 cm long with flaring lobes.

Leaves: Compound, elliptic to ovate, 5-10 cm long, finely divided into opposite leaflets.

Habitat: Dry open areas, roadcuts, roacky slopes, low to high.

Range: B.C. to Oregon.

SCROPHULARIACEAE · FIGWORT FAMILY

RICHARDSON'S PENSTEMON
Penstemon richardsonii

Plant: A taprooted, upright, multi-stemmed perennial, woody at the base, 20-70 cm tall.

Flower: Bright red, 2-3 cm long, in a few-flowered cluster at stem tips.

Leaf: All on stem, deeply toothed, 3-7 cm long and 1-3 cm wide.

Habitat: Dry, open, rocky places at lower elevations.

Range: B.C. to Oregon.

HOOD'S PHLOX
Phlox hoodii

Plant: A low, cushion-forming perennial to 6 cm high.

Flower: White, pink or bluish, the 5 petal lobes 4-7 mm long, flowers solitary at ends of stems.

Leaves: Small, linear, firm, sharp, 4-10 mm long and about .5 mm wide, with hairy edges.

Habitat: Dry, open places in plains and foothills, commonly with sagebrush.

Range: Alaska to Oregon.

SHOWY PHLOX
Phlox speciosa

Plant: An upright perennial from a woody base, 10-40 cm tall.

Flower: Pink to white, 2-3 cm wide, the petals almost always notched at the tip.

Leaves: Narrowly lanceolate, 3-7 cm long and .5-1 cm wide, opposite each other up the stems.

Habitat: Sage-steppe to ponderosa pine forest.

Range: B.C. to Oregon.

POLEMONIACEAE · PHLOX FAMILY

LONG-LEAVED PHLOX
Phlox longiflora

Plant: An erect perennial from a woody base, 10-40 cm tall.

Flower: Pink to white, the 5 petal lobes 7-15 mm long, flowers on short stems at stem ends.

Leaves: Opposite on stem, linear, 1.5-8 cm long and 1-2.5 mm wide.

Habitat: Dry, open, rocky places, from lowlands to midelevations in mountains.

Range: B.C. to Oregon.

63

HOOKER'S ONION
Allium acuminatum

Plant: A narrow, erect perennial 10-30 cm tall.

Flower: 5-30 pink flowers, each 8-15 mm long, gathered in a loose head at top of stem.

Leaves: 2 or more, long and narrow, shorter than flower head, withering as flowers appear.

Habitat: Dry hills and plains.

Range: B.C. to Oregon.

DAGGERPOD
Phoenicaulis cheiranthoides

Plant: A tufted perennial with basal leaves, 5-20 cm tall.

Flower: Petals pink or purple, 11-15 mm long , flowers on long stalks, seed pods 2-8 cm long.

Leaves: Oblanceolate and gray-hairy, 3-15 cm long, in rosettes.

Habitat: Sage-steppe and ponderosa pine forest.

Range: Washington to Oregon.

POLEMONIACEAE · PHLOX FAMILY

LINANTHUS
Linanthus pharnaceoides

Plant: A very fine-stemmed, delicate annual 3-30 cm tall.

Flower: 5 fused blue petals with yellow center, .5-12 mm wide.

Leaves: Compound, cleft into 3-9 whorled, linear segments 1-2 cm long.

Habitat: Sage-steppe to ponderosa pine forest.

Range: Washington to Oregon.

APOCYNACEAE · DOGBANE FAMILY

DOGBANE
Apocynum androsaemifolium

Plant: A branching perennial 10-50 cm tall.

Flower: Tubular flowers pinkish, 5-7 mm long, in loose clusters.

Leaves: Drooping, opposite on stem, ovate-elliptic, 2.5-7 cm long, often with a point at tip.

Habitat: Dry soil in open places from lowlands to midmountains.

Range: Throughout most of North America.

GEYER'S ONION

Allium geyerii

Plant: Narrow and erect, 10-50 cm tall.

Flower: Tepals pink, 4-10 mm long, heads with 10-25 flowers, occasionally replaced by small bulblets.

Leaf: 3 or more leaves per flower stem, 10-30 cm long and 1-5 mm wide, curved in cross-section.

Habitat: Moist meadows and along streams at lower elevations.

Range: Washington and Oregon.

STREAMBANK GLOBEMALLOW

Illiamna rivularis

Plant: A robust, upright perennial 1-3 m tall.

Flower: Rose-purple, the 5 petals 1.5-2.5 cm long, often slightly notched at tip.

Leaves: Mapleleaf-like, 5-15 cm long, generally 5-lobed and serrate.

Habitat: Streambanks, lakeshores and other moist areas at low elevations.

Range: B.C. to Oregon.

DESERT SHOOTINGSTAR

Dodecatheon conjugens

Plant: A tufted perennial 5-30 cm tall.

Flower: 1-10 flowers on a naked stalk, petals rose-pink and reflexed, 1-3 cm long, with a yellow tube in center.

Leaves: All basal, oblanceolate, 3-20 cm long and 2-5 cm wide.

Habitat: Moister areas in sage-steppe to montane meadows.

Range: B.C. to Oregon.

LONG-SEPAL GLOBEMALLOW

Illiamna longisepala

Plant: A branching-erect perennial 1-2 m tall.

Flower: Rose purple, 5 spreading petals about 2 cm long, sepals about 1.5 cm, in leaf axils.

Leaves: maple-like, 4-10 cm long and 5- to 7-lobed, alternate on stems.

Habitat: Sage-steppe to ponderosa pine forests.

Range: Central and southern Washington.

DIFFUSE KNAPWEED
Centaurea diffusa

Plant: A biennial 10-70 cm tall, stiffly branching and scratchy when mature.

Flower: Small white to pink composite heads, composed completely of disk flowers (no rays).

Leaves: Compound, 2-10 cm long, finely divided into narrow lobes.

Habitat: Dry, usually somewhat to very disturbed open areas.

Range: Native to the Mediterranean, now throughout the U.S.

BOUNCING BETT
Saponaria officinalis

Plant: A rhizomatous, leafy, spreading perennial 40-90 cm tall.

Flower: Many, the wedge-shaped petals white or pink, blade 10-15 mm long, indented at tip.

Leaves: Lanceolate, opposite each other on stem, 4-10 cm long and 1.5-4 cm wide.

Habitat: Usually on disturbed sites with plentiful moisture in spring.

Range: Native to Europe, now present throughout much of North America.

SCROPHULARIACEAE · FIGWORT FAMILY

ROSY OWLCLOVER
Orthocarpus bracteosus

Plant: A narrow, erect annual 10-40 cm tall.

Flower: Corolla 2 cm long, pink-purple, flowers crowded at stem tip.

Leaves: 1.5-3.5 cm long, narrow, the lower entire, the upper three-cleft.

Habitat: Meadows at low elevations.

Range: B.C. to Oregon.

COMPOSITAE · COMPOSITE FAMILY

CANADA THISTLE
Cirsium arvense

Plant: A perennial 30-150 cm tall that spreads abundantly from rhizomes.

Flower: Few to many purple, composite heads 1-3 cm across at top of upright stems.

Leaves: 5-20 cm long, deeply lobed and/or serrate, with thin spines along edges.

Habitat: Disturbed meadows and fields with saturated soil in spring.

Range: From Eurasia, now a noxious weed throughout North America.

HOARY CHAENACTIS, DUSTY MAIDEN
Chaenactis douglasii

Plant: Initially a rosette of leaves, then a narrow, erect biennial or perennial 10-60 cm.
Flower: Several white, non-showy composite heads on tall stalk, lacking ray flowers.

Leaves: 2-12 cm long, deeply divided into thick but very narrow lobes, fern-like.
Habitat: Dry, open, often sandy or rocky places, foothills to mountains.
Range: B.C. to Oregon.

COMMON BURDOCK
Arctium minus

Plant: A large biennial to 1.5 m tall.

Flower: Numerous pink composite heads 1-3 cm across, with disk flowers only.
Leaves: Basal and on flower stalks, broadly ovate, up to 30 cm long and 25 cm wide.
Habitat: Roadsides, fields, meadows, light shade, usually where there is some moisture.
Range: Native of Eurasia, now throughout temperate North America.

PINK MICROSTERIS
Microsteris gracilis

Plant: A diminutive annual 2-25 cm tall.

Flower: Pink, tubular, 5-15 mm long, the spreading petals 2-3 mm across, yellow within.

Leaves: Linear to elliptic, 1-5 cm long, 1-8 mm wide, often opposite below, alternate above.

Habitat: Steppe to ponderosa pine forest, sometimes where moist.

Range: B.C. to Oregon.

MARIPOSA LILY
Calochortus macrocarpus

Plant: A narrowly erect perennial to 20-50 cm tall.

Flower: 3 obovate, lavender petals with pointed tips, green at base bordered by a purple crescent.

Leaves: Linear, concave-channeled, alternate on stem and reduced upwards.

Habitat: Sage-steppe and dry grasslands.

Range: B.C. to Oregon.

MILKWEED
Asclepias speciosa

Plant: A rhizomatous perennial 40-120 cm tall, with milky juice.

Flower: Petals pink, reflexed, 8-12 mm, flowers 5-30 in rounded clusters.

Leaves: Oblong, 10-20 cm long and 5-10 cm wide, opposite one another up stem.

Habitat: Open or partially wooded sites with spring moisture.

Range: B.C. to Oregon.

FIELD MINT
Mentha arvensis

Plant: An erect, aromatic, rhizomatous perennial 10-70 cm tall.

Flower: Small, 4-7 mm long, white to pink, in clusters in axils of leaves.

Leaves: Elliptic, serrate, 2-8 cm long and 6-40 mm wide, opposite one another on stem.

Habitat: Moist places, especially along streams and lakeshores, low to moderate elevations.

Range: Alaska to Oregon.

PORTULACACEAE · PURSLANE FAMILY

BITTERROOT
Lewisia rediviva

Plant: A low, tufted perennial to 8 cm tall. Roots were an important Native American food.

Flower: Petals many (12-18), pink to white, oblanceolate, 18-35 mm long, stamens 30-50.

Leaves: All basal, narrow and succulent, 1.5-5 cm long by 1-3 mm, withering before bloom.

Habitat: Sagebrush to lower mountains, on dry, exposed, rocky soil.

Range: B.C. to Oregon.

PORTULACACEAE · PURSLANE FAMILY

TWEEDY'S LEWISIA
Lewisia tweedyi

Plant: A succulent, tufted perennial 10-20 cm tall.

Flower: 2-5 flowers per upright stem, 8-9 white to pink petals, 2.5-4 cm long, with 12-25 stamens.

Leaves: All basal, elliptic to obovate, 10-20 cm long and 2-5 cm wide, fleshy.

Habitat: On rocky slopes at edge of ponderosa forest.

Range: Central Washington.

NARROW-LEAVED COLLOMIA
Collomia linearis

Plant: A narrow, erect annual 10-50 cm tall.

Flower: Pink, blue or white, the corolla 8-15 mm long, flowers 2-10, clustered at top of stem.

Leaves: Narrowly lanceolate, 1-7 cm long by 1-13 mm wide, entire.

Habitat: Dry to somewhat moist open places from lowlands to midelevations.

Range: B.C. to Oregon.

HOPSAGE
Atriplex spinosa

Plant: A branching shrub up to 1.5 m tall, often with spiny twigs.

Flower: Tiny (1-3 mm) drab flowers bloom in axils of reduced leaves on an upright spike.

Fruit: Round winged seeds 8-15 mm across, white to red.

Leaves: Oblanceolate, 1-2.5 cm long, short-hairy.

Habitat: Foothills and desert valleys, often in alkaline soil.

Range: Washington to Oregon.

ROSY PUSSYTOES
Antennaria microphylla/rosea

Plant: A matted perennial 5-40 cm tall.

Flower: Clustered small white to rose compo-site heads at stem tip, resembling a cat's paw.

Leaves: Leaves mostly basal, oblanceolate, 8-30 mm long and 2-7 mm wide, gray-hairy.

Habitat: Dry, open places from the lowlands to high elevations.

Range: Throughout North America.

BIG-HEAD CLOVER
Trifolium macrocephalum

Plant: A rhizomatous perennial 5-30 cm tall.

Flower: Individual pink flowers 2-3 cm long, clustered in solitary heads 3-5 cm wide.

Leaves: Palmately compound, the leaflets 5-9, oblanceolate, .5-2.5 cm long, leathery.

Habitat: Sage-steppe to ponderosa pine forest, on rocky ground.

Range: Washington and Oregon.

75

WOOLLY-POD MILKVETCH
Astragalus purshii

Plant: A low, tufted, gray-woolly perennial 3-10 cm tall.

Flower: 1-3 cm long, yellow to purple, 3-10 flowers closely clustered at stem tips.

Fruits: 1-2.5 cm long, extremely white-woolly.

Leaves: Pinnately compound, gray-woolly, with 7-19 ovate-elliptic leaflets 5-20 cm long.

Habitat: Dry ground, sage-steppe to lower mountains.

Range: B.C. to Oregon.

GIANT HELLEBORINE
Epipactis gigantea

Plant: A rhizomatous perennial 30-100 cm tall.

Flower: Sepals coppery-green, 12-16 mm long, petals similar but thinner, in upper leaf axils.

Leaves: Elliptic, 7-17 cm long and 1.5-5 cm wide, sheathing the stem, veins parallel.

Habitat: Around springs and seeps, especially hot springs, also around lake margins.

Range: In much of western North America.

WEEDY MILKVETCH

Astragalus miser

Plant: A prostrate to erect perennial 10-50 cm tall.

Flower: Light pink-purple, 8-12 mm long, 3-15 flowers loosely grouped per stem.

Leaves: Compound, 3-16 cm long, with 9-17 variable leaflets, linear to oval, 5-30 mm long.

Habitat: Variable, on open ground and in partial shade from lowlands to alpine.

Range: B.C. to Washington.

CROUCHING MILKVETCH

Astragalus succumbens

Plant: A gray-hairy erect or spreading perennial, stems 10-50 cm long.

Flower: Pink, 18-26 mm, 10-20 flowers blooming together in a tight cluster in leaf axils.

Leaves: Compound, rather fleshy, 3-10 cm long, 13-19 oblong leaflets 3-15 mm long.

Habitat: Sagebrush plains to foothills.

Range: Central Washington to Oregon.

ROSACEAE · ROSE FAMILY

PURPLE AVENS
Geum triflorum

Plant: A spreading perennial forming clumps up to 30 cm broad, flower stems to 30 cm tall.

Flower: Bowl-shaped, with pink to yellow petals and purple sepals, in clusters of 1-5.

Leaves: Mostly basal, obovate, 5-15 cm long, deeply cleft and toothed in feathery segments.

Habitat: Moister spots in the sagebrush plains to subalpine ridges.

Range: Throughout North America.

COMPOSITAE · COMPOSITE FAMILY

RUSH-PINK
Stephanomeria tenuifolia

Plant: A scraggly, milky-juiced perennial 20-70 cm tall.

Flower: Dainty, pink 5-petaled flowers (these are actually small composite heads) bloom at branch tips.

Leaves: Linear to filiform (thread-like), 1 to 8 cm long and .5-3 mm wide.

Habitat: Dry, often rocky places from plains to midelevations.

Range: B.C. to Oregon.

STICKY GERANIUM
Geranium viscosissimum

Plant: A branching perennial 20-70 cm tall.

Flower: Pink, petals 14-20 mm long, rounded at the tip, hairy at base, with dark penciling.

Leaves: 5-12 cm wide, deeply lobed, such that leaves look like a hand, the lobes serrate.

Habitat: Meadows with some spring moisture, plains to pine forest.

Range: B.C. to Oregon.

STORK'S-BILL, FILAREE
Erodium cicutarium

Plant: A small, tufted annual 3-30 cm tall.

Flower: Flowers pink, 10-15 mm across, seed pod elongates to form 2-5 cm stork's bill.

Leaves: Mostly basal, compound, leaflets opposite and deeply incised.

Habitat: Dry, often disturbed areas at low to moderate elevations.

Range: Native to Eurasia, now throughout western North America.

79

SELF-HEAL
Prunella vulgaris

Plant: A low perennial with one to several stems, prostrate or erect, 5-40 cm long.

Flower: Blue-violet, 1-2 cm long, flowers in short, dense spikes 20-50 cm long at stem tips.

Leaves: Ovate-elliptic leaf 2-9 cm long and 1-4 cm wide, the margins entire or vaguely toothed.

Habitat: In moist, open places from lowlands to midelevations in mountains.

Range: Throughout North America.

RAGGED ROBIN
Clarkia pulchella

Plant: An upright or branching annual 10-50 cm tall.

Flower: 4 rose-purple petals, each with 3 very distinct lobes and a narrow base.

Leaves: Linear to spoon shaped, 2-7 cm long, alternate on the stem.

Habitat: Dry, open places in the lowlands and foothills.

Range: B.C. to Oregon

SCROPHULARIACEAE · FIGWORT FAMILY

SHRUBBY PENSTEMON
Penstemon fruticosus

Plant: A low shrub 10-40 cm tall.

Flower: Blue-lavender, 3-5 cm long, in showy upright clusters at stem tips.

Leaves: Numerous, elliptic, toothed or entire, 3-6 cm long and .5-1.5 cm wide.

Habitat: Dry, open, often rocky places, low to high elevations.

Range: B.C. to Oregon.

SCROPHULARIACEAE · FIGWORT FAMILY

GAIRDNER'S PENSTEMON
Penstemon gairdneri

Plant: A low shrub with several stems 10-40 cm tall from a woody base.

Flower: Blue-purple to rose-purple, 14-22 mm long, 2-12 flowers in loose spikes at top of stem.

Leaves: Linear, entire, alternate on stem, 3-7 cm long and 1-3 mm wide.

Habitat: Dry, open, mostly rocky places, often with sagebrush.

Range: Washington and Oregon.

LEGUMINOSAE · PEA FAMILY

SILKY LUPINE
Lupinus sericeus

Plant: One to several-stemmed, gray-hairy perennial 20-50 cm tall.

Flower: Blue-purple, 10-12 mm long, in uncrowded spikes 5-15 cm long.

Leaves: All on stem, palmately compound, the 7-9 oblanceolate leaflets 3-6 cm, silky-hairy.

Habitat: Sage-steppe to openings on ponderosa pine forest.

Range: B.C. to California.

CRUCIFERAE · MUSTARD FAMILY

PURPLE CROSSFLOWER
Chorispora tenella

Plant: An upright to sprawling annual weed 5-40 cm tall, branching at the base.

Flower: 4 purple petals, the visible portion of each about 5 mm long, flowers on upper stem.

Fruits: Narrow, curved pods 3.5-4.5 cm long.

Leaves: Elliptic to oblanceolate, 3-8 cm long, the edges sinuate (wavy).

Habitat: Dry, disturbed sites at lower elevations.

Range: From Eurasia, now throughout the arid portion of the Pacific Northwest.

SULFUR LUPINE
Lupinus sulphureus

Plant: A branching perennial 30-70 cm tall.

Flower: 9-12 mm long, and strange to say, the flowers are yellow on some plants and purple on others.

Leaves: Palmately compound, with leaflets 9-11, those 2.5-4 cm long, hairy at least below.

Habitat: Sage-steppe, grasslands and ponderosa pine.

Range: B.C. to Oregon.

VELVET LUPINE
Lupinus leucophyllus

Plant: A gray-woolly perennial 30-70 cm tall.

Flower: Lilac to pale lavender, 8-12 mm long, in crowded spikes 10-20 cm tall.

Leaves: All on stem, palmately compound and gray-hairy, 7-10 narrow leaflets 3-5 cm long.

Habitat: Sage-steppe and dry foothills to ponderosa pine forest.

Range: Washington to Oregon.

COMMON CAMAS
Camassia quamash

Plant: An upright perennial 20-70 cm tall, typically colonial (many plants crowded together).

Flower: Blue to violet, 6 tepals 15-35 mm long, 8-30 flowers clustered on upright stem.

Leaves: Flat, 10-40 cm long and 8-20 mm wide.

Habitat: Moist open areas that are dry by summer.

Range: B.C. to California.

WHITE-STEMMED FRASERA
Frasera albicaulis

Plant: Erect perennial with tufted leaves and several stems 10-70 cm tall.

Flower: Purple, 4 sepals, 4 petals, 4 stamens, petals spreading, 5-11 mm, ciliate at base.

Leaves: Basal and opposite on stem, linear-oblanceolate, conspicuously 3-nerved, 5-30 cm.

Habitat: Meadows and forest openings, plains to midelevations.

Range: B.C. to Oregon.

NAKED BROOMRAPE
Orobanche uniflora

Plant: A diminutive, non-photosynthetic plant parasitic on many species, including saxifrage, 3-10 cm tall.

Flower: Purple or occasionally yellow, tubular, 13-20 mm long, the 5 lobes ciliate-hairy.

Leaves: reduced to a few yellow bracts on stem.

Habitat: Open places, moist to dry, and open woods, lowlands to midmountains.

Range: Throughout North America.

PURPLE MILKVETCH
Astragalus agrestis

Plant: A low, spreading perennial 10-30 cm tall.

Flower: Purple, 13-18 mm long, with 7-20 flowers together in a tight, upright cluster.

Leaves: Compound, hairy, 4-10 cm long, 11-19 linear to lanceolate leaflets 1-2 cm long.

Habitat: Moist open areas from sagebrush to alpine slopes.

Range: B.C. to Oregon.

85

SAGEBRUSH VIOLET
Viola trinervata

Plant: A tufted perennial 5-15 cm tall.

Flower: 10-15 mm long, bicolored, upper petals reddish, lower ones lilac.

Leaves: 1.5-4 cm long, stiff, palmately incised into lobes, the lobes also sometimes incised.

Habitat: Sage-steppe and rocky hillsides.

Range: Washington and Oregon.

WILD MOUNTAIN MINT
Monardella odoratissima

Plant: A low, matted perennial from a woody base, 10-50 cm tall.

Flower: 5 assymetrically arranged, purple-to-white petals are fused together at the base, numerous flowers packed together in tight heads at stem tips.

Leaves: The elliptical leaves are opposite one another on the stem, 1-3.5 cm long.

Habitat: Dry, open, rocky places from the lowlands to midelevations in mountains.

Range: B.C. to California.

BALLHEAD WATERLEAF

Hydrophyllum capitatum

Plant: A soft-hairy perennial 5-40 cm tall.

Flower: Purple, 5-9 mm long, stamens protruding, flowers crowded in rounded clusters among leaves.

Leaves: Ovate, 5-15 cm by 5-10 mm, deeply divided into lobes, which are again incised.

Habitat: In deciduous thickets and edges of lowland forests.

Range: B.C. to Oregon.

CHECKER LILY

Fritillaria lanceolata

Plant: A narrow, erect perennial 15-80 cm tall.

Flower: Purple with yellow-green mottling, 6 lanceolate tepals 2-3 cm long, flowers pendent.

Leaves: 1 or 2 whorls of 3-5 on stem, plus several solitary, lanceolate, 5-15 cm by 3-25 mm.

Habitat: Prairies, grasslands and conifer woods.

Range: B.C. to Oregon.

87

BLUE LETTUCE
Lactuca pulchella

Plant: An erect, branching perennial 20-100 cm tall.

Flower: Blue, with 18-50 ray flowers in a composite head, flowers in loose cluster.

Leaves: Lanceolate-elliptic, 5-18 cm long, 6-35 mm wide, lower with lobes, upper ones entire.

Habitat: Meadows, thickets and other moist places at lower elevations.

Range: Alaska to Oregon.

DOUGLAS BRODIAEA
Brodiaea douglasii

Plant: A narrow, erect perennial 20-70 cm tall.

Flower: Blue, tubular, 9-14 mm long, the tepals with wavy margins, 3-15 flowers at top of stem.

Leaves: 1-2 leaves, 25-50 cm long and 3-10 mm wide, flat but keeled below.

Habitat: Grasslands and sagebrush to ponderosa pine forest.

Range: B.C. to Oregon.

CAMPANULACEAE · HAREBELL FAMILY

COMMON DOWNINGIA
Downingia elegans

Plant: An ascending annual 5-40 cm tall.

Flower: 1 in each upper leaf axil, 4-10 mm long, blue to pink, with yellow-ridged white eye.

Leaves: All on stem, elliptic, .5-2.5 cm long, .2-1 cm wide, sessile, borders entire.

Habitat: Vernal pools, wet meadows, pond edges.

Range: Washington to California.

SCROPHULARIACEAE · FIGWORT FAMILY

BLUE-EYED MARY
Collinsia parviflora

Plant: A delicate annual 1-25 cm tall.

Flower: Blue with white on upper lip, 4-8 mm long, in leaf axils and at stem tip.

Leaves: Opposite on stem, narrowly elliptic, 1-5 cm long and 4-12 mm wide.

Habitat: Dry, open places from lowlands to moderate elevations in mountains.

Range: Alaska to Oregon.

GRAY BALL SAGE
Salvia dorrii

Plant: Branching-erect shrubs 10-50 cm tall.

Flower: Blue-violet, 7-12 mm long, stamens protruding, flowers in clustered whorls on upper stems.

Leaves: Elliptic to oblanceolate, 1.5-3 cm long and 4-15 mm wide, short-hairy.

Habitat: Dry, open places in plains and foothills, often with sagebrush.

Range: Washington to Oregon.

LONG-FLOWERED BLUEBELL
Mertensia longiflora

Plant: A small perennial 5-25 cm tall.

Flower: 2-10 tubular blue flowers clustered at stem end and pendant, each 1.5-2.5 cm long.

Leaves: Few, mostly on stem, oblanceolate, 20-60 cm long and .5-3 cm wide.

Habitat: Sage-steppe and ponderosa pine forest.

Range: B.C. to southern Oregon.

BORAGINACEAE · BORAGE FAMILY

BLUE STICKSEED
Hackelia micrantha

Plant: A robust, branching perennial 20-100 cm tall.

Flower: Corolla blue with a yellow or white eye, 7-11 mm wide, flowers usually numerous.

Leaves: Oblanceolate to elliptic, 5-35 cm long and 1-4 cm wide, long-hairy.

Habitat: Forest openings and meadows.

Range: B.C. to Oregon.

HYDROPHYLLACEAE · WATERLEAF FAMILY

NARROW-LEAVED PHACELIA
Phacelia linearis

Plant: An erect annual 5-40 cm tall, may be branching or not.

Flower: 5 fused blue-lavender petals 8-18 mm across, turning whitish at the base.

Leaves: All on stem, narrow, 1.5-11 cm long and 1.5-12 mm wide, some with flaring lobes.

Habitat: Dry, open places in foothills and plains.

Range: B.C. to southern Oregon.

CHELAN PENSTEMON
Penstemon pruinosus

Plant: Sub-shrub (woody base) 10-40 cm tall.

Flower: Deep blue, 11-16 mm long, flowers clustered in discrete whorls on stem.

Leaves: Elliptic to spear-shaped, usually serrate, 5-12 cm long and 1-2 cm wide.

Habitat: Dry, open places at lower elevations, often with sagebrush.

Range: B.C. and Washington.

SHARP-LEAVED PENSTEMON
Penstemon accuminatus

Plant: A several-stemmed perennial 15-60 cm tall.

Flower: Bright blue, 14-21 mm long, 5-10 flowers in distinct clusters on stem.

Leaves: Oblanceolate, thick and firm, edges entire, 5-15 cm long and 1-2 cm wide.

Habitat: Dry, open, sandy places at low elevations.

Range: Central Washington to Oregon.

COMMON LARKSPUR

Delphinium nuttallianum

Plant: An erect, single-stemmed perennial 15-50 cm tall.

Flower: Blue to white, lower sepals (which are petal-like) 17-25 mm, spur 13-20 mm, 3-15 flowers.

Leaves: Few and mostly basal, 2-6 cm long, palmately compound with linear segments.

Habitat: Sage-steppe to ponderosa pine forest, into mountains.

Range: B.C. to Oregon.

WILD BLUE FLAX

Linum perenne

Plant: A woody-based perennial 10-60 cm tall.

Flower: Petals blue-purple, 1-2 cm, flowers persist for only one day.

Leaves: Linear, 1-3 cm long, 1-nerved, alternate up stem.

Habitat: On dry, sandy soil from prairies to alpine ridges.

Range: Throughout western North America.

Index of Common and Scientific Names